ACET **fb** BOOKS

corporate personality in ancient israel

H. WHEELER ROBINSON

BIBLICAL SERIES

FACET BOOKS

BIBLICAL SERIES

F A C E T **fb** B O O K S

BIBLICAL SERIES – 11

John Reumann, General Editor

Corporate Personality in Ancient Israel

by H. WHEELER ROBINSON

FORTRESS PRESS   PHILADELPHIA

"The Hebrew Conception of Corporate Personality" was first published in *Werden und Wesen des Alten Testaments: Vorträge gehalten auf der Internationalen Tagung Alttestamentlicher Forscher zu Göttingen vom 4.-10. September 1935*, ed. P. Volz, F. Stummer, and J. Hempel ("Beihefte zur Zeitschrift für die Alttestamentliche Wissenschaft." 66; Berlin, 1936), and is reprinted here by arrangement with the publisher, Alfred Töpelmann.

"The Group and the Individual in Israel" was first published in *The Individual in East and West* (ed. E. R. Hughes, 1937), and is here reprinted by arrangement with the publisher, Oxford University Press, Inc.

Printed in U.S.A.   7799G64   UB3011

Introduction

FEW topics have come to pervade modern biblical studies as has the Hebrew conception of "corporate personality." The classic (and pioneer) presentation of this topic is a paper read in 1935 by the British Baptist scholar H. Wheeler Robinson. Though published in English and frequently referred to, the essay has not been widely read, perhaps because it originally appeared in Germany in a rather inaccessible volume, which was printed as a supplement to a learned journal. Facet Books now makes this important article available to a wider audience, and with it another, more popular but even lesser known lecture delivered by the same author in 1936, "The Group and the Individual in Israel." Together the two provide an excellent introduction to that important Semitic complex of thought in which there is a constant oscillation between the individual and the group—family, tribe, or nation—to which he belongs, so that the king or some other representative figure may be said to embody the group, or the group may be said to sum up the host of individuals.

The author of these two essays, Henry Wheeler Robinson, is almost as intriguing as the topic he treats. Born on February 7, 1872, at Northampton in central England, he was raised by his mother and at the age of fifteen had to leave school to go to work in the countinghouse of a Northampton leather merchant. After his baptism in 1888, he distinguished himself as a Sunday school teacher, and soon he preached his first sermon. He continued to study in evening classes and began to contribute articles to a local Nonconformist magazine. Encouraged by friends, in 1890 he entered Regent's Park College, the Baptist training school in London, to study for the ministry.

Ten years of study followed, in London, at Edinburgh University (1891-95), then at Mansfield College, the Congregational theological school in Oxford, and at the continental universities of Marburg and Strassburg, where young Robinson attended the classes of such Old Testament scholars as Karl Budde and Theodor Nöldeke. He had shown special ability in Semitic studies, and while at Mansfield College where he worked particularly under George Buchanan Gray, he was awarded several prizes, especially for his work on terms in Hebrew psychology.

Setting academic promise aside, he accepted a call to a Baptist congregation at Pitlochry, Scotland, where he settled with his bride in 1900. In 1903 he was persuaded to move to St. Michael's Baptist Church in Coventry, a difficult situation which demanded sturdy faith as well as decided tact; nonetheless in his three years there membership in the small congregation rose substantially. During these years in the parish Robinson showed himself a careful preacher, an exacting teacher, and a dedicated scholar. His midweek services and Sunday Bible classes brought teaching opportunities at which he lectured on an astonishing range of topics; out of one such series of lectures grew his later book *The Cross of Job*.

In 1906 Robinson was called to Rawdon Baptist College outside Leeds, where he at first taught almost everything except Old Testament. By 1914, in addition to his college duties, he was lecturing at the University of Leeds. During the wartime emergency in 1917, he added to his already considerable burdens by assuming charge of a local congregation. Nevertheless a steady stream of books and articles issued from his pen during these years. There were commentaries on Deuteronomy and Joshua (in the *Century Bible*, 1907), Jereiah, Obadiah, and Micah (in *Peake's Commentary*, 1919), nd articles for the *Encyclopaedia Britannica's* famed eleventh dition (1910), Hastings' *Dictionary of the Apostolic Church*, nd Hastings' *Encyclopaedia of Religion and Ethics*. He pro- uced the first edition of his *The Christian Doctrine of Man* 1911); a book, still in print, on *The Religious Ideas of the*)ld *Testament* (1913); numerous articles in denominational apers; and a treatise on Baptist principles that was later ranslated into German and Danish. To carry this work load e arose at 5 A.M., tutored his children before breakfast, and ften ended the day in his study at 2 A.M. It is small wonder hat such labors drove his body to a near fatal collapse in 1913. ut out of the ordeal of illness came a concern for the meaning f suffering which was to be reflected in several books, begin- ing with *The Cross of Job* (1916). There emerged too an ver increasing interest in the work of the Holy Spirit. It is haracteristic of Wheeler Robinson's approach that before ublishing his famous book on the Holy Spirit he set up a lan that supplemented scholarly analysis of biblical texts with roup experience. He invited six friends to join him in an xperimental seminar which called for half a year's preliminary :udy of a syllabus on the topic of the Holy Spirit followed by :ssions that involved the participants in corporate devotions nd reflections on their own Christian experience. Later .obinson took advantage of the corporate thinking offered in :ssions with pastoral associations to develop further his ieology of the Spirit.

New demands on Robinson's time came when he was elected rincipal of Regent's Park College in 1920. Here he was able) fulfil a dream from his own student days of locating a aptist theological college in the environment of one of ritain's two great universities. In 1926 the decision was made) move Regent's Park College to Oxford. The Old Testament :holar now found himself not only an administrator but also fund-raiser, and that in the depths of a depression. Although e and his family moved to Oxford in 1927, for ten years he ommuted between there and London, teaching at both places

until 1938 when the cornerstone was laid for the new Regent
Park College, construction of which was opportunely com
pleted just as World War II began. In the opinion of hi
biographer, Ernest Payne, the college in Oxford will alway
be H. Wheeler Robinson's "chief memorial."

Once again Robinson's many duties did not diminish hi
literary output. An essay published in 1925 testified to hi
continuing interest in Hebrew psychology, and a book o
Baptist history published in 1927 reflected his role as a leade
in his church and as president of the Baptist Historical Society
Lectures on "The Cross of Jeremiah" and "The Cross of th
Servant" were published in 1925 and 1926 respectively, and
further volume on the problem of suffering in 1939. His boo
on the Holy Spirit appeared in 1928, a dozen years after th
experimental seminar. An intensely personal book in th
sphere of devotional literature, *The Veil of God,* came out i
1936. His many contributions to Old Testament study in
cluded *The History of Israel,* which was published in 193
and is still being reprinted. Robinson's interest in systemati
theology is evidenced in his last two books, *Redemption an
Revelation in the Actuality of History* (1942) and *Inspiratio
and Revelation in the Old Testament* (published posthumousl
in 1946). The former book may be said to be the climax o
Robinson's great trilogy consisting of *The Christian Doctrin
of Man* (1911), *The Christian Experience of the Holy Spir*
(1928), and *Redemption and Revelation* (1942).

Editorial work also claimed much of Robinson's time. Be
tween 1927 and 1942 fifteen volumes in the "Library of Con
structive Theology" (of which he was coeditor) passed ove
his desk. For the two symposia which he edited, *Record an
Revelation* (1938) and *The Bible in its Ancient and Englis
Versions* (1940), he also provided significant essays. *Recor
and Revelation* was undertaken for the British Society fc
Old Testament Study, of which he was a past president.

Solid learning, wide intellectual interests, deep piety—thes
are the traits remembered by Robinson's students and assoc
ates. A man with a fantastic zeal for work, he took fe

acations, although he did enjoy reading detective stories, a
assion shared by many other theologians. He early realized
the potentialities of religious broadcasting, then in its infancy,
nd spoke on the radio on more than one occasion. Christians
eyond his own communion knew him not only through his
writings but also through his participation in the ecumenical
movement; church unity, he believed, would best be shown
t the Lord's table and in the Spirit's work. Robinson is said
o have made some of his deepest personal impressions on
udents through his Saturday morning sermon classes and
rough the Friday evening communion services which he
nstituted at Regent's Park College. In 1942, on his seventieth
irthday, he was honored with a volume of essays by his
ormer pupils and colleagues, and that spring retired from
ne college. Though he continued to lecture at Oxford and
lsewhere, in the three years that remained of his retirement
ailing health precluded the realization of some of his fondest
reams, including a projected theology of the Old Testament.
Ie died on May 12, 1945, three days after the end of the war
n Europe.

What concerns us here in the work of Wheeler Robinson
s the development of his understanding of corporate per-
onality. During his student days at Mansfield College he had
written an essay on Hebrew psychology for George Buchanan
Gray, which he later expanded into a dissertation on "The
'sychological Terms of the Hebrews"; this dissertation, sub-
nitted while he was at Pitlochry, won Robinson the Senior
Kennicott Hebrew Scholarship at Oxford in 1901. Out of this
tudy grew the paper on "Hebrew Psychology in Relation to
'auline Anthropology" which he contributed in 1908 to the
volume of *Mansfield College Essays* honoring A. M. Fairbairn.
'airbairn (1838-1912), a noted Congregationalist theologian,
nad encouraged and furthered Robinson's career at several
points; Robinson's essay in his honor opened up new aspects
n biblical and theological investigation. It contains *in nuce*
ome of the ideas later developed in the two essays printed
nere and, though many of its points are now commonplaces

of biblical study, it ought to be read as background to thes
essays.

In the essay honoring Fairbairn, Robinson sought to sho
that "Paul, a Hebrew of the Hebrews, is primarily and char
acteristically Hebrew in his anthropology, and that even wher
his ideas (in this realm) come nearest to a Greek form or ar
clothed in a Greek terminology, they are a legitimate outcom
of Old Testament conceptions" (p. 268). Such a Hebrai
background of Pauline theology is by now widely concedec
but in a period when Paul was being interpreted almost ex
clusively in light of Greek mystery cults, Wheeler Robinso
was striking a new note. He carefully analyzed Old Testa
ment terms like "soul" (*nephesh*) and "spirit" (*ruach*), an
then showed how Paul uses Greek words to express an essen
tially Hebraic anthropology. Ideas which reappear in a mor
developed form in Robinson's later writings are broache
here: that animism stands behind Hebrew psychology; tha
man is no "immortal soul imprisoned in a body" but an inter
reaction of "breath-soul," spirit, and the body with its variou
organs, that he is in short "an animated body," to use th
phrase that Robinson employed later; and that the Christia
is essentially the product of the divine Spirit to whom h
has yielded himself. The essay concluded that the trunk o
Pauline anthropology is formed by Hebrew psychology anc
that, although Paul transforms each Old Testament concept
he does so without taking grafts from Hellenism (p. 285).

These lines of thought, only sketchily stated in 1909, ar
worked out in more detail in later articles, notably in th
several editions of *The Christian Doctrine of Man* and in a
essay on "Hebrew Psychology" published in 1925. The firs
essay in this Facet Book represents the real flowering of thes
years of investigation. It was read to the Second Internationa
Congress of Old Testament Scholars at Göttingen in Septem
ber, 1935. Robinson had had ties with German biblical scho
larship ever since his student days, and after World War
was chosen as the representative of British scholarship t
contribute a paper to the German periodical *Zeitschrift fü*

ie *alttestamentliche Wissenschaft,* and thus to help re-estab-
sh the ties the war had severed. The Congress in 1935
ttracted some eighty-five biblical scholars, including such
aminaries as Alt, von Rad, Baumgärtel, Augustin Bea (the
uture Cardinal), Eissfeldt, Weiser, Rowley, and T. H. Robin-
on. In this galaxy Wheeler Robinson's address stood out
onetheless. Johannes Hempel remarked that it was "for
nany of us an advance into a new land" (*Zeitschrift für die
lttestamentliche Wissenschaft,* XII [1935], 303), although
Robinson admittedly built on much that he had said previously as well as on the work of Johannes Pedersen in Den-
mark and the parallel but independent investigations of Otto
Eissfeldt (cf. p. 17, n. 63 below).

The following year Robinson was asked to participate in a
ecture series for Oxford undergraduates on the individual in
arious societies. His presentation on "The Group and the
ndividual in Israel," published in an anthology in 1937 and
eprinted here, thus appeared in the broader setting of study
of the individual in primitive society, Chinese thought,
Hinduism, and so forth. The change of audience accounts
or the absence of Hebrew terms, the dearth of scholarly
pparatus, and the more far-reaching allusions. The setting
lso accounts for the fact that Robinson addresses himself at
he close to the bearing which his study had on the present-
lay world, something all the lecturers were asked to do;
ence also the care with which Robinson, in the world of
936, distinguished "corporate personality" from "collec-
ivism." It is noteworthy, however, that in a series on the
ndividual Robinson begins with the primary place of the
group; this is true to his societary emphasis. However, the
very theme of the individual compels him to state in more
letail and with greater clarity what he had noted as point
"4" of his 1935 essay but had not developed there, since
e regarded it as something obvious to the professional scho-
ars of that day. Since the later essay, on "group and individual," gives a more balanced picture of the whole subject,
t might well be read first, especially if the pages on "corpo-

rate personality" prove too intricate at first reading. It is i
the 1935 address to Old Testament scholars, however, tha
the more careful foundations are laid.

Since 1936, of course, debate about Wheeler Robinson
theses on the group and the individual has continued. H
own books, notably *Redemption and Revelation* and *Inspir*
tion and Revelation, often allude to the conception. Edmon
Jacob has rightly called his essay a "classical formulation,
but agreement has not been total by any means. Of th
specific applications which Robinson suggested in 1935, tha
involving the figure of the Servant in Deutero-Isaiah has bee
especially debated. Robinson had suggested that the lon
dispute over whether "the Servant" is some historical indi
vidual or represents instead the nation Israel might be resolve
by recognizing the oscillations of corporate personality
While some sort of "collective theory," usually associate
with this concept of personality, seems the most attractiv
view today (according to the surveys of C. R. North), i
must be added that scholars of the Scandinavian school, suc
as Lindblom and Engnell, who approach such problems i
light of the community and its cult and of a king and futur
Messiah figure, make little use of the corporate personalit
theory. Other scholars, like Eichrodt, believe that an indi
vidual is intended.

With regard to Robinson's application of corporate per
sonality to the use of the pronoun "I" in the Psalms—a prob
lem long debated by the exegetes—it must be confessed tha
recent discussion of such psalms by no means agrees that a
application of the corporate personality idea solves the prob
lem. In his commentary on the Psalms Artur Weiser return
to the view set forth by Balla in 1912 that the "I" of individua
laments does refer to an individual person and not to th
community speaking with a single voice; Weiser adds, how
ever, that the individual speaks in the context of the cult o
the covenant festival, so that the "I" is not to be interprete
in terms of modern individualistic piety.

In New Testament study there have been other application

of corporate personality, often along lines hinted at by Robinson. T. W. Manson, for example, makes use of the concept of corporate personality in explaining some of the "Son of man" sayings in the Gospels; the "church" or "people of God" theme is implicit in Jesus' teachings, says Manson. And one of the possible backgrounds of the Pauline concept of the church as "the body of Christ" continues to be the corporate personality idea.

Both essays are here reprinted very much as Robinson first published them. A few obvious misprints have been corrected, punctuation and capitalization have been altered to conform to American usage, the footnotes have been numbered consecutively for each essay, and the Hebrew words have been transliterated according to the system employed in Pedersen's *Israel*, a book which Robinson quotes several times in the first essay. The bibliographical information in Robinson's footnotes is often scanty; thirty years after the publication of the essays it is necessary to identify more fully works which were familiar to Robinson's fellow scholars. This information has been supplied by the editor. The translations appearing in brackets have also been provided by the editor, as has other material that appears in brackets. All biblical quotations seem to be cited either from the Revised Version of 1881-85 or in Robinson's own translation; they have been left in their original form. In some cases such quotations of course agree with the King James Version or, strikingly, anticipate the Revised Standard Version.

Full bibliographical data for all titles noted in this Introduction will be found at the end of the book in the section "For Further Reading."

JOHN REUMANN

Lutheran Theological Seminary
Philadelphia
March, 1964

Contents

THE HEBREW CONCEPTION
OF CORPORATE PERSONALITY

In the terminology of English law, "corporation" denotes either "a body corporate legally authorised to act as a single individual," or "an artificial person created by royal charter, prescription, or legislative act, and having the capacity of perpetual succession." [1] Both usages are covered by the Hebrew conception of corporate personality, though without the necessity for any legal prescription. The larger or smaller group was accepted without question as a unity; legal prescription was replaced by the fact or fiction of the blood-tie, usually traced back to a common ancestor. The whole group, including its past, present, and future members, might function as a single individual through any one of those members conceived as representative of it. Because it was not confined to the living, but included the dead and the unborn, the group could be conceived as living for ever.

No one can overlook this unity of corporate personality in its more legal aspects. Familiar examples from the Old Testament are given when Achan breaks the taboo on the spoil of Jericho, and involves the whole of Israel in defeat

[1] *Shorter Oxford English Dictionary*, s.v.

and, on discovery, the whole of his family in destruction;[2] or when seven of Saul's descendants are executed to expiate the Gibeonite blood shed by Saul;[3] or in the practice of Levirate marriage, which (on any explanation of its origin) points to a unitary group conception;[4] or in the responsibility of a whole city for murder or heathenism within its area;[5] or in the belief that Yahweh visits the iniquities of the fathers upon the children;[6] or in the practices of the blood-feud, before it was limited by the *lex talionis*.[7] Such examples are very familiar. They have to be admitted because they found expression in external acts. They presuppose a conception of the family or clan very different from the group ideas of today. The modern man usually starts from the rights of the individual; English law, for example, warrants the removal of the child from the control of the father, where its individual claims are at stake.[8] This, of course, is in direct opposition to the ancient *patria potestas;*[9] in modern times a son might feel morally bound to pay his father's debts, but in the ancient world he would often have been sold as a slave to pay them.

It is, however, not only in Hebrew law that the conception operates, but also in ways much less easy to detect, because they have found less open expression. They are often important for the exegesis of the Old Testament, and will be

---

[2] Josh. 7. Such social solidarity is found throughout the world wherever there is a primitive but socially organized group; cf. A. H. Post, *Afrikanische Jurisprudenz*, p. 49. For other examples see M. Löhr, *Sozialismus und Individualismus im Alten Testament* (Giessen, 1906), *passim;* Otto Procksch, *Über die Blutrache bei den vorislamischen Arabern* (Leipzig, 1899).

[3] II Sam. 21.

[4] Deut. 25:5 ff.; cf. J. M. Mittelmann, *Der altisraelitische Levirat* (Leipzig, 1934), p. 7.

[5] Deut. 13:12 ff., 21:1 ff.

[6] Exod. 20:5.

[7] Gen. 4:15, 24; Exod. 21:23-25.

[8] *Encyclopaedia Britannica, s. v.* "Children-Protective Laws." The Children Act was passed in 1908.

[9] Judg. 11:34 ff.; Jer. 32:35; Deut. 21:18 ff., etc.

illustrated in the second part of this paper. But it is necessary first to glance at certain aspects of the conception itself. Four of these call for special notice, viz., (1) the unity of its extension both into the past and into the future; (2) the characteristic "realism" of the conception, which distinguishes it from "personification," and makes the group a real entity actualized in its members; (3) the fluidity of reference, facilitating rapid and unmarked transitions from the one to the many, and from the many to the one; (4) the maintenance of the corporate idea even after the development of a new individualistic emphasis within it.

(1) The extension of the living family to include its ancestors, or, as we should rather say, the extension of the ancestors to include the living members of the family, is best expressed in the familiar phrases about being gathered to one's fathers, or going to one's fathers, or to one's kindred.[10] Thus Jacob says, "I am to be gathered unto my kindred; bury me with my fathers" (Gen. 49:29). This shows that burial in the family sepulcher is the realistic act which unites a man with his ancestors. If he is not properly buried, this unity is not properly achieved. No doubt it is difficult for us to reconcile this burial in a grave with the conception of Sheol, except by thinking of Sheol as an assemblage of all the graves. Thus in Ezekiel (32:17-32), the shades of Sheol are depicted in groups according to different nationalities and fortunes. Yet as Pedersen [11] reminds us, Sheol is not the mere sum of the separate graves. "All graves have certain common characteristics constituting the nature of the grave, and that is Sheol. The 'Ur'-grave we might call Sheol; it belongs deep down under the earth, but it manifests itself in every single grave as *mō'ābh* manifests itself in every single Moabite. Where there is grave, there is Sheol, and where there is Sheol, there is grave." We notice also that both Samuel and Joab

---

[10] Gen. 15:15, 25:8, 49:29; Num. 27:13.
[11] J. Pedersen, *Israel: its Life and Culture*, I-II (Copenhagen: Branner, and London: Oxford University Press, 1926), p. 462.

are buried in their own houses.[12] This illustrates the common belief that the ghost remained in specially close relation to the grave in which the body had been buried.[13]

There is a similar extension of the living group into the future as part of its unity. This is best illustrated by the dominant aspiration of the Hebrew to have male children to perpetuate his name, the name that was so much part of himself that something of him died when his name ceased. It was as much of a misfortune to have no male children as to miss the proper burial rites. "Man is only what he is as a link in the family."[14] Thus what Robertson Smith has said of the living group may be extended both before and after. "A kin was a group of persons whose lives were so bound up together, in what must be called a physical unity, that they could be treated as parts of one common life. The members of one kindred looked on themselves as one living whole, a single animated mass of blood, flesh and bones, of which no member could be touched without all the members suffering."[15]

Along such lines, then, the corporate personality of the family, the clan, and the people was conceived realistically as a unity, a unity which made possible the all-important doctrine of election, and lent unity to the history itself. Amos can address his contemporaries in the eighth century as still "the whole family which I brought up out of the land of Egypt,"[16] since they are both its representatives and its actual constituents. The people *are* their ancestors, as the patriarchal narratives often illustrate. The conception of history as a

[12] I Sam. 25:1; I Kings 2:34.
[13] E. g., Rachel, Jer. 31:15 (cf. I Sam. 10:2).
[14] Pedersen, *op. cit.*, p. 259. Cf. II Sam. 14:7.
[15] W. Robertson Smith, *Lectures on the Religion of the Semites* (new ed., rev.; London: A. and C. Black, 1894), pp. 273-74. We may compare Isa. 58:7, "hide not thyself from thine own flesh," and Rom. 11:14, where Paul speaks of the Jews as "my flesh."
[16] Amos 3:1.

unity derives in the last resort through Christianity from the Hebrew prophets and apocalyptists, and they are working with the unity of corporate personality. We may still speak of the unity of a nation's history, but we mean something very different from the ancient concrete conception. *We* mean the immanent evolution of its characteristic; *they* meant that concrete realism which has been exhibited.

(2) This realism is itself a second characteristic point of difference between ancient and modern ideas. The Hebrew conception is neither a literary personification nor an ideal. Its study does not belong to the linguistic, but to the archeological and anthropological sides of the subject. It is an instinctive and not a consciously made unification. Pedersen brings that out forcibly when he speaks of the individual Moabite (*mōʾābhi*) as a manifestation of the type (*mōʾābh*), "which is the sum and substance of Moabitic features," acting as a unity and treated as such.[17] In the light of such considerations, a deeper meaning is given to the detailed individualistic portraiture of such passages as describe the national history through the life-story of an unchaste woman in Ezekiel 16 and 23,[18] or through that of a forsaken and barren but now restored wife, the mother of many children, in Isaiah 54:1 ff. An impressive example is afforded by the passage in Daniel 7:13, 27, where the human figure coming with the clouds of heaven is explicitly identified as the people of the saints of the Most High. This means that their unity is so realistically conceived that it can be concentrated into a single representative figure. If we ask on what this unity is based, the answer for the Semites at least is doubtless that of the common blood-tie, whether real or fictitious (as by a blood covenant or some form of adoption), rather than of the cult of a common an-

[17] *Op. cit.*, p. 109.

[18] Eissfeldt points out that the individualizing traits here go beyond anything we find in the description of the Servant of Yahweh (*Einleitung in das Alte Testament* [Tübingen: J. C. B. Mohr, 1934], p. 382; 2nd ed. [1956], p. 412).

cestor—though this itself also expresses the unity. But quite definitely we must *not* think of anything like Rousseau's rights of man and voluntary social contract. Nor must we think of a merely ideal or figurative existence of Rachel, when the prophet depicts her as weeping for her children by the family graves;[19] Rachel weeps because she dies in her children. Still further, we must note the relation of this conception of corporate personality to that of individual personality, as shown by the psychological ideas of the Hebrews. For them, the personality consisted of a number of bodily organs animated by a breath-soul and each possessing a diffused and distributed psychical and ethical quality. It is precisely the same idea which belongs to the unity of the group. The group possesses a consciousness which is distributed amongst its individual members and does not exist simply as a figure of speech or as an ideal. Indeed we may generalize to the extent of saying that there is usually a close parallelism between the psychology of the individual and the conception of society which prevails in any age. We may see it in Plato's *Republic*, through his close comparison of the individual and the state.[20] We may see it in the Pauline description of the church [21] as the "body of Christ." We may see it also in the biological ideas of modern times as applied both to the individual and to the social organism. Perhaps it is inevitable, since the only unity we can know directly is that of our own consciousness, so that our way of conceiving this will always tend to be reflected in our view of society.

(3) The fluidity of transition from the individual to the society and *vice versa* can be most easily illustrated from levels of consciousness far below those of the Old Testament, and

[19] Jer. 31:15.

[20] *Republic*, ii. 369: "the counterpart of the greater as it exists in the form of the less"; iv. 435: "there exist in each of us the same generic parts and characteristics as are found in the state" (Eng. trans. by Davies and Vaughan).

[21] I Cor. 12:12 ff. Cf. *Ep. ad Diognetum*, 6: "The soul is spread through all the members of the body."

especially from totemistic groups. (These more primitive conceptions have, of course, been sublimated in the Old Testament ideas, like the taboo-conception of holiness, or like the symbolic magic which underlies the symbolic acts of the prophets.) The group conception in primitive thought has been specially studied by Lévy-Bruhl [22] and by Durkheim, [23] in relation to the Australian aborigines. The former writer calls this conception "the law of participation," by which he means that "things, beings, and phenomena can be in a manner incomprehensible for us, at once themselves and something other than themselves." [24] This quasi-mystical identification he notes as one of the outstanding characteristics of pre-logical mentality. "It permits the primitive mind to think at the same time of the individual in the collective and the collective in the individual." [25] "Each individual *is* at one and the same time such and such a man, or such and such a woman, actually alive, such an ancestral individual (human or semi-human) who lived in the mythical times of the *Alcheringa*, and at the same time he *is* his totem, i.e., he participates mystically in the essence of the animal or vegetable species of which he bears the name." [26] It is not suggested that the Hebrews passed through such a totemistic stage, but simply that such absence of the sharp antitheses familiar to us is psychologically possible. But if so, then transitions from the one to the many and from the many to the one were much easier for them than for us.

We may illustrate the same kind of transition, worked out in a long development, from the religion of the ancient

[22] *Les Fonctions Mentales dans les Sociétés Inférieures* (1910), Eng. trans. L. A. Clare, *How Natives Think* (New York: Knopf, 1926).

[23] *Les Formes Élémentaires de la Vie Religieuse* (Paris, 1912), Eng. trans. Joseph Ward Swain, *The Elementary Forms of the Religious Life* (London: G. Allen and Unwin, and New York: Macmillan, 1915).

[24] *Les Fonctions Mentales*, p. 77.

[25] *Ibid.*, p. 100.

[26] *Ibid.*, p. 94; cf. Durkheim, *Les Formes Élémentaires*, pp. 336 ff.

Egyptians. Wolf [27] has recently suggested that the absence of a consciousness of sin and the need of redemption, in spite of the Osirian judgment of the dead, is due to the absence of self-conscious individuality. It was the people as a whole, represented by the divine king, who had to do with God. Only when absolute kingship replaced representative kingship, towards the end of the Middle Kingdom, was there sufficient disintegration for more direct relation of the individual with Osiris; but then the religion possessed no creative force. The parallel and contrast with Israel's development of individualism is obvious, for there the transition led to the richest development of the religion. In all the generations there is this interplay of sociality and individuality, for they both belong essentially to our human nature. But in the ancient world they were much more closely and subtly blended than in the more self-conscious modern, and so it was possible to combine both, or to pass easily from one to the other.

(4) In accordance with this general principle, it is quite wrong to place the individualism of Jeremiah and Ezekiel in direct antithesis to the group conception which had hitherto prevailed. The group conception still remained dominant, notwithstanding the extreme consequences as to moral and religious responsibility which Ezekiel draws from his individualistic emphasis;[28] we have only to think of his vision of a restored and regenerated community [29] to see this. So with his forerunner Jeremiah. The prophecy of the New Covenant[30] stands for the multiplication of the prophet's own consciousness of God, when all the Lord's people shall be prophets; yet it is a covenant with Israel as a nation, like the old covenant, however different its method. The later development of the eschatology shows that the complete destiny of

[27] Walther Wolf, *Individuum und Gemeinschaft in der ägyptischen Kultur*, pp. 17-21.

[28] Ezek. 18.

[29] Chaps. 37 and 40 ff.

[30] Jer. 31:33-34; cf. (at a lower level) Num. 11:29; Joel 3:1-2 [in Eng. trans., Joel 2:28-29].

the individual can be realized only if the nation accomplishes its own.[31] In the later Judaism, as Moore points out,[32] " 'a lot in the World to Come' . . . is ultimately assured to every Israelite on the ground of the original election of the people by the free grace of God." The individualizing development takes place within the matrix of a social relation to God.[33] On the other hand, it is equally wrong to emphasize the social relation in the earlier period to the point of neglecting the fact of individual religion and morality. It must have been true that the earlier prophets, addressing Israel as a nation, and challenging it to repentance, or even simply condemning its sins, were in some degree thinking in terms of the individual Israelite. In fact, as we have just seen from Jeremiah, the new individualism was a product of the individual religious experience of the prophets, which must inevitably lead them to individualize within the collective mass which they formally addressed. This must have been reinforced by the response of their disciples, itself creating a new group within the larger unit, and prophesying a new Israel.[34] But even so, the prophets are not to be assimilated to the journalist, the politician, and the preacher of today, addressing individuals in order to form a new community within state or church. The prophets always worked within the larger unity of Israel, and from Israel in the mass towards Israel as found in its most worthily representative Israelites.

[31] Adolphe Lods, *Les prophètes d'Israël et les débuts du judaisme* (Paris, 1935), p. 375; Eng. trans. S. H. Hooke, *The Prophets of Israel and the Rise of Judaism* (London: Routledge and Kegan Paul, 1937), p. 331.

[32] George Foot Moore, *Judaism in the First Centuries of the Christian Era: The Age of the Tannaim* (Cambridge: Harvard University Press, 1927-30), II, 94-95.

[33] Even the late individualism of Job passes easily into the universal experience of suffering, and shows what Eissfeldt calls *die kollektivistische Verhaftung des jüdischen Individuums* ["the confining of the individual in Judaism within the collective"] (*Einleitung in das Alte Testament, op. cit.*, p. 516; 2nd ed., p. 571).

[34] Isa. 8:16; cf. Mal. 3:16-17.

So far, we have considered the more general aspects of the conception of corporate personality, and it has been suggested that this affects the whole relation of Israelites to one another and to Yahweh. It is, of course, impossible to attempt any exhaustive review of its applications. They would range from the accidence and syntax of Hebrew grammar up to the highest levels of Old Testament theology. It is not fanciful to see the collective emphasis in the apparent priority of collective nouns to those which represent units (cf. *ç'ōn,* ["flock"], and *seh,* ["one of a flock"]),[35] in the unity of idea which underlies the use of the construct state, and in the use of such words as *nephesh* ["breath," "spirit," or "soul"], *lēbh* ["heart"], *dām* ["blood"] in the singular with plural suffixes.[36] On the other hand, the fundamental conception of the covenant (*b'rīth*), which can be made the basis of a complete theology of the Old Testament,[37] is inseparably linked to the conception of corporate personality. For our present purpose, however, it must suffice to select three outstanding types of application, all of great and wide importance for exegesis, viz., the representation of the nation by some outstanding figure belonging to it; (2) the individual-collective nature of the "I" of the Psalms and of the "Songs of the Servant of Yahweh"; (3) the character and content of Hebrew morality as the right relation of individual members of the group to one another.

(1) In the first place, the conception throws light on the peculiar prominence of individual personalities both in the

---

[35] Carl Brockelmann, *Kurzgefasste vergleichende Grammatik der semitischen Sprachen* ("Porta Linguarum Orientalium," 21; Berlin: Reuther and Reichard, 1908), p. 209.

[36] Cf. W. Robertson Smith, *Kinship and Marriage in Early Arabia* (Cambridge University Press, 1885), p. 40: "The whole kindred conceives itself as having a single life, just as in the formula 'our blood has been spilt' it speaks of itself as having but one blood in its veins."

[37] As by Walther Eichrodt, in his very useful *Theologie des Alten Testaments;* 3 parts (Leipzig: J. C. Hinrichs, 1933-39); trans. J. A. Baker from the 6th German ed. (1959), *Theology of the Old Testament, Volume One* ("The Old Testament Library"; Philadelphia: Westminster, 1961).

making of Hebrew history and in the development of Hebrew religion.[38] At first sight, this may seem a paradox, when we are stressing the community sense. Yet it is a paradox only in appearance. Where the corporate sense is strong, the outstanding man will gather to himself the force of the whole group. Thus T. E. Lawrence can say of modern Bedouins, "Among the Arabs there were no distinctions, traditional or natural, except the unconscious power given a famous sheikh by virtue of his accomplishment," whilst in another place he can characterize the Semites as "the race of the individual genius." [39] In the patriarchal narratives of Genesis the great ancestors of Israel, Abraham, Isaac, and Jacob, are a remarkable blend of the typical Israelite with the nation, and thus fittingly its representatives, since as S. A. Cook remarks, "Hebrew thought refers with equal facility to a representative individual or to the group he represents." [40] When the monarchy emerges, the king is Yahweh's son, which is exactly what Hosea calls the nation.[41] The king represents the people to Yahweh; he was, in C. R. North's words, "a Priest in and through whom the people were brought near to God, rather than a Prophet through whom God was mediated to the people." [42] The priestly representation of the community is illustrated by the judgment scene at which Joshua the high priest is acquitted.[43] Similar identification occurs with prominent laymen, such as Nehemiah: "I confess the sins of the children of Israel, which we have sinned against thee; yea, I and my father's house have sinned." [44] Similarly, the prophet owes his peculiar place as an intercessor with God,[45] to the fact that he temporarily becomes the nation, and makes its

[38] H. Wheeler Robinson, *The Religious Ideas of the Old Testament* (London: Duckworth, 1913), pp. 20-21.

[39] *Seven Pillars of Wisdom* (Garden City, New York: Doubleday, Doran, and Co., 1935), pp. 39, 157.

[40] *Cambridge Ancient History* (New York: Macmillan, 1923-39), III (1925), 493.

[41] II Sam. 7:14; Hos. 11:1.

[42] "The Religious Aspects of Hebrew Kingship," *Zeitschrift für die alttestamentliche Wissenschaft*, Neue Folge, IX (1932, Heft 1), 37.

[43] Zech. 3:1–10.   [44] Neh. 1:6.   [45] E.g., Amos 7:2, 5.

needs articulate. The profound sympathy of the prophet with the people whose doom he may have to foretell owes not a little to this corporate identity—"for the hurt of the daughter of my people am I hurt." [46] The principles of prophetic "symbolism" enabled a prophet to see the corporate significance of the individual. Thus it might be claimed that Hosea's relation to Gomer is not merely a private and personal affair made into a dramatic analogy; Gomer in both her sin and her anticipated repentance *is* the nation of which she is an actual sample and an epitomizing and representative unit. Later on, the Maccabean martyrs consciously identify themselves with the nation. [47] The principle of vicarious suffering which they exemplify and articulate is itself an application of social solidarity, in which it may be said to be latent. [48] In truth, the higher purpose of any group is always expressed by a minority within it, sometimes a minority of one. Yet the one or two remain the representatives of the group for the time being. We may compare the repeated transference of the theme of a symphony from one instrument or group of instruments to another; for the time being, each leads and represents the values of the whole orchestration. The most familiar of all examples of this representative value is seen in the thoroughly Hebraic contrast of Adam and Christ made by the Apostle Paul, which draws all its cogency from the conception of corporate personality: "as in Adam all die, so also in Christ shall all be made alive." [49]

(2) In the second place, our discussion of corporate personality bears on the much-debated question of the "I" of the Psalms and of the Servant of Yahweh. In regard to the Psalms, the collective interpretation which was urged by Smend in

[46] Jer. 8:21.   [47] II Macc. 7:38; IV Macc. 6:28-29, 17:21-22.
[48] S. A. Cook, *op. cit.*, p. 491.
[49] I Cor. 15:22. T. W. Manson, in *The Teaching of Jesus* (Cambridge University Press, 1931), p. 227, has argued that the term "Son of man" in the Synoptic Gospels is itself a corporate conception, linked with that of the Old Testament.

888,[50] and found wide acceptance in the early years of this entury, seems to have given way to the individualistic view resented by Balla in 1912,[51] and largely employed by Gunkel 1 his commentary on the Psalms (1926).[52] On the other hand, Mowinckel[53] has emphasized what he calls "community mysti- ism," and applied it specially to the cult, remarking that "the onception of the community as a 'great ego' is genuinely emitic—and genuinely primitive—, and makes itself felt par- icularly in the cult where the *communio sanctorum* emerges s a body and a soul." In this view he sees the element of truth 1 the argument of Smend, to which, as he says, Balla has not aid sufficient attention. The fact is that the conception of orporate personality for which we have argued largely re- noves the sharp antithesis between the collective and the ndividualistic views. Smend himself to some degree saw this, s when he says *so liegt dabei zunächst wenigstens keine hetorische oder poetische Figur vor, die mit Bewusstsein esucht würde. Es handelt sich hier vielmehr um einen ganz nwillkürlichen Ausdruck des Gemeingefühls.*[54] Balla does not

---

[50] "Über das Ich der Psalmen," *Zeitschrift für die alttestamentliche Wissenschaft*, VIII (1888), 49-147.

[51] *Das Ich der Psalmen* ("Forschungen zur Religion und Literatur des Alten und Neuen Testaments," 16; Göttingen, 1912).

[52] Especially *Einleitung*, pp. 173-75 (1928). [*Einleitung in die Psalmen: Die Gattung der religiösen Lyrik Israels* ("Göttinger Handkommentar zum Alten Testament," Ergänzungsband; Göttingen: Vandenhoeck & Ruprecht, 1933). The commentary referred to above is *Die Psalmen, übersetzt und erklärt* ("Göttinger Handkommentar zum Alten Testament," II Abteilung, Vol. II, 4th ed.; Göttingen: Vandenhoeck & Ruprecht, 1926).—EDITOR.]

[53] S. Mowinckel, *Psalmenstudien* (Oslo, 1921-24; reprinted, Amsterdam: P. Schippers, 1961), Buch I, pp. 164-65; cf. Buch V, pp. 36-38, Exkurs. [Cf. also Mowinckel's discussion in *The Psalms in Israel's Worship*, trans. D. R. Ap-Thomas (2 vols.; New York: Abingdon, 1962), specially pp. 42 ff.—EDITOR.]

[54] *Op. cit.*, p. 60. ["What we have then, in the first instance at least, s not a consciously contrived rhetorical or poetical figure. We are onfronting, rather, a completely instinctive expression of communal eeling."—EDITOR.]

meet this when he speaks[55] of *das regellose Hinundhersch
wanken zwischen einem Ich und Wir* as being without an
psychologisch-ästhetische Begründung. Nor is Gunkel an
nearer the mark when he dismisses the collective view wit
contempt as *ein letzter Rest der früher allgemeingültige
allegorischen Deutung der heiligen Schrift* and says that it
psychologically impossible for the "I" of the poet to pass int
the "I" of the community.[56] It is *not* psychologically impos
sible in view of the examples given, and a similar usage undei
lies the undeniable applications of Hebrew law. Moreovei
the view we have presented is neither allegory nor personifica
tion, but a primitive category of thought which is ver
different from our own antithesis of the collective and th
individual. The writer of a psalm is indeed always an indivi
ual and not a syndicate, and there is a sense in which it ma
be said that every psalm does represent an individual exper
ience and outlook. It is also unnatural for a psalmis
consciously to imagine himself as a community. But if th
collective sense is so much a part of himself and of his outlool
as it was with the Israelite, then he can never wholly detacl
himself from the social horizon. The absence of our sharpe
distinctions and different starting-point will be seen in tha
fluidity of movement which has been emphasized; in Psalm 44
for example, there are no less than six transitions from th
singular to the plural or from the plural to the singular. Thi
is the poetic equivalent of many prose passages, such as th
speech of Israel to Edom,[57] "We will go up by the high way
and if we drink of thy water, I and my cattle, then will I giv

[55] *Op. cit.*, pp. 133-34. ["... the irregular shifting back and fortl
between 'I' and 'we'" is without any "psychological-aesthetic founda
tion."—EDITOR.]

[56] *Einleitung in die Psalmen, op. cit.*, p. 175. ["... a final vestige o
the allegorical sense previously applied everywhere to Holy Scrip
ture ..."—EDITOR.]

[57] Num. 20:19, on which see G. Buchanan Gray, *Numbers (Interna
tional Critical Commentary;* New York: Scribner's, 1903), pp. 265-66
he points out "that the characteristic and original names of nations ar
singulars—Moab, Edom, Israel, Midian, Jerahme'el."

Dear Librarian:

We regret that we cannot supply

catalog cards for this particular

title.

BRO-DART BOOKS, INC.
P.O. Box 923
Williamsport, Penna.

he price thereof." How is this different from Psalm 44:6-7
Eng. trans., 5-6]: "Through thy name will we tread them
under that rise up against us. For I will not trust in my bow"?
To explain this transition as Balla does[58] by reference to a
supposed leader suddenly thinking of himself, is most unnatural, whereas the fluid conception of corporate personality
at once supplies an adequate explanation, based, as Mowinckel
rightly says,[59] "not on the external fact of representation
through a single person, but on primitive psychology."

All that has been said about the "I" of the Psalms of course
applies to the even more keenly debated question as to the
identity of "the Servant of Yahweh" in Deutero-Isaiah. The
great variety[60] of views which have been maintained by emi-
nent scholars, and not less the oscillation[61] of the views of
those scholars themselves, is provocative of thought. Does it
not suggest that the central issue, that between a collective
and an individualistic interpretation, is being argued on an
antithesis true to modern, but false to ancient modes of
thought? To us there certainly seem to be data for both views
in the "Songs," even apart from their contexts. But we have
seen that the Hebrew conception of corporate personality can
reconcile both, and pass without explanation or explicit indi-
cation from one to the other, in a fluidity of transition which
seems to us unnatural. In the light of this conception the
Servant can be both the prophet himself as representative of
the nation, and the nation whose proper mission is actually
being fulfilled only by the prophet and that group of followers
who may share his views. To say this is not to take refuge
in a vague and ambiguous formula, though the formula may
be difficult enough to express and apply in translation and

[58] *Op. cit.*, pp. 108-9.
[59] *Psalmenstudien, op. cit.*, Buch V, p. 37.
[60] Conveniently tabulated by P. Volz, *Jesaia II übersetzt und erklärt* "Kommentar zum Alten Testament," IX, 2; Leipzig: A. Deichertsche Verlagsbuchhandlung, 1932), p. 167. The identifications with out-standing individuals almost parallel Ben Sirach's catalog of the famous men of Israel, or the roll call of the heroes of faith in Hebrews 11.
[61] E.g., Duhm, Sellin, Gunkel, and Mowinckel.

exegesis. Ancient literature never does fit exactly into our categories.

Let us rapidly review the four "Songs" from this standpoint. In the first (Isa. 42:1-4) the mission of the Servant is to the "nations" (*gōyim*) of the earth, and such an international mission suggests national activity by the people Yahweh has chosen. Even if none yet shared this outlook with the prophet, his consciousness of it is instinctively nationalistic. He conceives Israel as meekly accepting its national suffering, and active through its missionary propaganda. The individualizing features do not go beyond those of the normal Hebrew imagination, e.g., as applied elsewhere to Babylon (47:1-3), or Zion (54:1-2).

In the second Song (49:1-6), the prophet-Servant is burdened with the sense of the blindness and deafness of the actual Israel (42:19), and says, "I have toiled in vain"; but he is encouraged by the promise of a wider mission than that of converting his own nation—that world-mission which requires indeed a converted nation for its fulfilment. This is just the sort of paradox in which religion delights; a man is strengthened for a smaller task by being shown a larger one. The movement of thought in vss. 5 and 6 is from the smaller to the larger mission of the Servant;[62] the prophet's consciousness, and with it his conception of the Servant's mission and the connotation of the name, expand through the conversion of his fellow Israelites to the fulfilment of the national mission. The prophet is conscious of no contrast during that expansion. He *is* Israel created to be the Servant; he is Israel, though working alone to make Israel what she ought to be; he is Israel finally become a light of nations to the end of the earth. This seems to be better described as "realism" than as a contrast of the "ideal" collective personality and the "real"

[62] It is more natural to take *lᵉshōbhēbh* ["to bring back"], etc. as referring to the *'ebhedh* ["Servant"] and not as a gerundial expression of Yahweh's purpose in *'āmar* [the Lord "says"]; but this does not really affect the above argument.

ndividual.[63] The English term "ideal" is a dangerous one to
use of a people so realistic in their thinking as Israel. The
scope of actuality expands or contrasts in the way suggested,
but never passes beyond what imagination actualizes as "real,"
whether in the one or the many. In the third Song (50:4-9),
he Servant is strengthened against suffering by fellowship
with God, whether the opposition encountered be Jewish or
Gentile. Because of divine help he is confident that his mission
will be fulfilled. Here too the experience of God is individual,
whilst the mission for God is collective; Hebrew thought is
content to bring them into juxtaposition, because corporate
personality could reconcile both. In the fourth Song (52:13—
53:12), it is Israel as a whole—now restored to its former home
and so vindicated—on which the many nations gaze in
wonder.[64] The past sufferings of the exile are now seen in a
new light; they were thought to be deserved penalty, but
they are really vicarious suffering for the nations themselves
in a larger solidarity; they have become, in fact, a sacrificial
offering (*'āshām*) through which the nations can approach
Yahweh.[65] This has come about because the prophet's spirit
has become that of the nation and because Yahweh has vindicated the faith of his Servant by a national resurrection from
the grave of exile. The double *motif*, i.e., the national mission
and the individual vocation, is thus carried through to the
end, and it is made possible for Hebrew thought by the recon-
ciling principle of corporate personality.

[63]Cf. Eissfeldt, *Der Gottesknecht bei Deuterojesaja (Jes. 40-55) im
Lichte der israelitischen Anschauung von Gemeinschaft und Individuum*
(Halle, 1933), p. 25; Eng. trans., "The Ebed-Jahwe in Isaiah xl.-lv. in the
Light of the Israelite Conceptions of the Community and the Individual,
the Ideal and the Real," *The Expository Times*, XLIV (1933), 261-68.
I am in general agreement with his argument, which makes a use of
corporate personality similar to that outlined above, but independently
of my book *The Cross of the Servant* (London: SCM, 1926), in which
it was presented.

[64] Cf. Ps. 126:2 for a similar Gentile attitude.

[65] The only textual difficulty is *'ammi* in 53:8, which must be read as
ammīm (cf. Lam. 3:14, where there is good support from manuscripts
and the Syriac for correcting the same error).

(3) We have seen how the principle works in the repre
sentation of the group by the individual, and in the expansio
of the individual consciousness to that of the group; we ma
now glance at its working within the group in the relation o
its members to one another. This is the field of Hebrev
morality, limited[66] and yet intensified by the sense of corporat
personality. As S. A. Cook says, "Ethical ideas are at leas
implicit in the group-idea, for the social group protected it
poor and weak members—provided the group-sentiment wa
strong." [67] It is interesting to compare Hebrew ethics witl
those of the Greeks, more individualized because springin
from the idea of an artificial state, and based on the relatio
of the individual to social traditions and political order.[6
Greek ethics was concerned with life as a whole—"the har
monious adjustment of the elements in man's nature—materia
and spiritual, individual and social," [69] whereas the cruder an
narrower outlook of the Hebrews derived from its nomadi
period. T. H. Robinson has well said of Israel, "She brough
with her from the nomad stage a conception of commo
brotherhood which she was the first to apply to the condition
of a highly organized settled community . . . to every othe
ancient monarch the subject was a slave, to the Israelite kin
he was a brother." [70] When we look back to those nomadi
conditions, as for example they are depicted in Doughty'
Arabia Deserta, we see at once the nomadic strain in the classi
cal epitome of prophetic morality—"to do justice and to lov
mercy." [71] Doughty says, "in the opinion of the next governe

[66] Cf. G. Buchanan Gray, *The Divine Discipline of Israel* (London
A. and C. Black, 1900), p. 46.

[67] *Op. cit.*, p. 439.

[68] Cf. John Dewey and J. H. Tufts, *Ethics* (New York: Henry Holt
1908), p. 111.

[69] J. H. Muirhead, "Ethics," in *Encyclopaedia of Religion and Ethics*
ed. James Hastings (Edinburgh: T. and T. Clark, and New York
Scribner's, 1908-27), V (1912), 422.

[70] *Palestine in General History* (Schweich Lectures for 1926; Oxfor
University Press, 1929), pp. 41 and 44.

[71] Mic. 6:8.

ountries, the Arabs of the wilderness are the justest of
mortals" and "In the hospitality of the Arabs is kinship and
assurance, in their insecure countries. This is the piety of the
Arab life, this is the sanctity of the Arabian religion, where
we may not look for other." [72] In close relation to this is the
law of blood-feud, which is the true measure of effective
kinship. [73] If we take such cross sections of the development
of Hebrew morality as are afforded, say, by the Book of the
Covenant, the Law of Holiness (Lev. 19) and Job's *apologia
pro vita sua* (chap. 31), it is easy to see the presence of both
justice and mercy throughout, and their development within
the group. If *mishpāṭ* stands for the original element of tribal
custom, *ḥesed* represents that mingling of duty and love which
brings directly from the conception of common ties, and
expands to include and regulate the conception of Yahweh's
relation to Israel, so uniting morality and religion in the most
characteristic feature of all Israel's development. We do not
exaggerate when we say that Hebrew morality, and conse-
quently Christian morality, are what they are because they
sprang up within a society dominated by the principle of
corporate personality.

If the argument of this paper is sound, its theme is of considerable importance for the interpretation of the Old Testament, and deserves more attention than it has received. Again
and again, we have to put ourselves back to a view of things
very different from our own. A good and interesting example
of this may be borrowed from Wolf's account [74] of Egyptian
art. Egyptian wall-paintings show the absence of all perspective and a stereotyped rectangular view of the subject. This, he
argues, is the unconscious result of that community-emphasis of
which Egypt is so striking an example. On the other hand, perspective drawing in the full sense did not come in till our own

[72] C. M. Doughty, *Travels in Arabia Deserta* (Cambridge University
Press, 1888), I, 249; II, 152.

[73] W. Robertson Smith, *Kinship and Marriage in Early Arabia, op. cit.*,
22.

[74] *Op. cit.*, pp. 7-16. This brief study is of great interest.

Renaissance times, and was itself connected with the rise of modern individualism, since perspective always implies a particular and individualized point of view. Thus the ancient drawings in the flat would be something like the popular ballad or myth, a product of the corporate personality of Egypt, a view of things as all might see them. The illustration is a useful one to remember, for it may remind us always to get back from our own modern standpoint to that more corporate and social view of things which is so striking a feature of the Old Testament.

THE GROUP AND THE
INDIVIDUAL IN ISRAEL

AT THE OUTSET of any historical survey of the rela-
ons of society and the individual, and particularly of those
ithin Israel, there are three general considerations which
eserve to be mentioned. The first is that there can never be
ny ultimate and exclusive antithesis of the two. The individ-
al could not come into existence at all without some form of
ociety, and depends upon it for his growth and development.
he society finds articulate expression only through the in-
ividuals who constitute it. Human personality is in itself as
uly social as individual. Differences of emphasis will be felt
a different periods, and it seems generally true that a pre-
ominant consciousness of the group precedes the fuller
iscovery of the individual. But it would be wrong to suppose
nat in the earlier period of Israel's history, for example, there
as little or no consciousness of the individual; the point is
ather that the individual was then *more* conscious of being
ne of the group. It would be equally wrong to suppose that,
a the later period, the greater sense of individuality altogether
xcluded the consciousness of membership in a corporate

unity. In all the generations, past and present, the systole an the diastole of both individuality and sociality are heard the heartbeats of humanity.

The second point is that there was much more fluidity the ancient conception of both the group and the individu so that one could merge into the other much more easily th our modern categories allow. Thus the society could fir realistic incorporation in an individual who represented it, su as the king or priest, and the individual instinctively enlarg his own consciousness so as to speak confidently in the nan of the whole group, as does the prophet and the psalmist Israel.

The third point is that in the interpretation of the conten porary social order, the individual tends to project his ow idea of himself. The subjectivity which we see in Rousseau *Confessions* passed into the individualism of his *Social Contra* and the theories which so influenced the French Revolutio Indeed, it often seems that it is the psychology of an a which shapes its sociology. Thus Plato explicitly makes t ideal state parallel in its elements with those of the individu person: "In each of us there are the same principles and habi which there are in the State," [1] i.e., the rational, the spirite and the appetitive. The Hebrew psychology, on the oth hand, started not with an indwelling soul, but with animated body, each of its physical members having psychic and ethical qualities. Personality was a "United States" rath than an empire. In correspondence with this psychology t Hebrew society (in spite of its monarchical governme during part of its history) is of essentially democratic cha acter, very conscious that each of its members has rights his own.

With these considerations in mind, we shall review: (1 The primary place of the Group in Israel; (2) The emergen of the Individual through the prophetic consciousness; (; The Jewish and the Christian Synthesis of this individualis into new group-unities.

[1] *Republic*, iv. 435, Jowett's translation.

THE PRIMARY PLACE OF THE GROUP

The essentially democratic character of Hebrew society
)es back to, and derives from, its nomadic period. The Book
' Deuteronomy (chap. 26) contains a liturgy of thanksgiving,
 which the Israelite looks back across the basket of first fruits
 : is presenting to Yahweh and humbly acknowledges that
\ wandering Aramean was my father" [Deut. 26:5]. There
 e links with that nomadic past in the familiar stories of the
 itriarchs and of the wanderings after the Exodus from Egypt;
 id to that idealized past the great prophets return to gain a
 proachful background for the sorry present. But the actual
 ory of that past must have been much simpler and cruder
 an is represented in the stories and traditions; its real nature
 ay be seen from such a book as Doughty's *Arabia Deserta*,
 hich describes the little-changed Bedouins of the nineteenth
 ntury.[2]

The nomadic clan must have been large enough to defend
 ielf, and on occasion to attack other groups, yet not so large
 to outrun the water supply at the oases in its range of
 urneyings. Its tie was one of blood, real or assumed, except
 ·r the protected "foreigners" who were of necessity attached
 · it—since the desert is no home for the isolated individual.
 he protective principle of the clan was that of blood-
 venge, by which each member of the group was pledged to
 :act vengeance, for a wrong done to his fellow, from mem-
 :rs of the group to which the offending man belonged. It
 a nomad's boast of blood-revenge that is preserved for us in
 The Song of Lamech" (Gen. 4:23-24):

> Hear my voice, O wives of Lamech,
>   listen to my word;
> A man do I slay for my bruise,
>   and a child for my stripe.

[2] C. M. Doughty, *Travels in Arabia Deserta* (Cambridge University
 ess, 1888).

> For seven times shall Cain be avenged,
> But Lamech seventy times and seven.

From such unrestricted vendetta which magnifies th
offence and multiplies its victims from the hostile clan, it
a real advance in morality to reach the *lex talionis* of Israel
first code of law in Canaan (Exod. 21:24-25), viz., "woun
for wound, stripe for stripe," instead of many wounds (
stripes for one.

The nomad clan continued to be the effective group un
even after the settlement of the Israelites in Canaan: Davi
is represented as asking Jonathan's permission to be away from
court that he may attend the annual sacrifice of his clan i
Bethlehem (I Sam. 20:6). Such a clan would contain a num
ber of what *we* should call "families"; on the other hand,
group of clans tracing by genealogy a more distant blood
connection constituted in theory the "tribe." In theory, fo
the familiar "tribes of Israel," sprung from the twelve sons o
Jacob, are a genealogical fiction. The actual grouping o
Israelites into such larger units was due rather to geographic
settlement, mixed marriages, conquest or assimilation of othe
groups, including the Canaanites themselves and groups o
Israelites who probably settled in Canaan directly from th
desert without sharing in the experiences of the Exodus.

If we would picture the normal group-life of the Israelit
settled in Canaan, we must think primarily of a limited num
ber of families gathered in a village or small town. Th
common sacrificial meal to which Samuel invited the youthf
Saul had thirty guests (I Sam. 9:22); we may assume th
these were the "elders," the heads of the families composir
the village. The communal affairs would be in the hands (
these elders, who met to discuss them "in the gate." Such
scene is well described for us in the Book of Ruth (chap. 4
when Boaz arranges to take over the rights and duties of th
nearest kinsman of Naomi, in order that he may marry th
widowed daughter-in-law of Naomi. Ten elders are chose
the business is discussed; a symbolic action marks its decisio

d the bystanders with the elders are called to witness it.
he incident may be taken to illustrate not only the communal
e of the village or town, but also the quite subordinate place
women in the social order. They were the property of
eir father or their husband who would naturally represent
em and defend their interests; but widows and orphan boys
girls who had no relative to take their part "in the gate"
ere an easy prey for the oppressor. That is why we hear
many admonitions from lawmakers or prophets to defend
d help these classes left without representative defenders.
he same thing applies to "the stranger within thy gates,"
t we should note that this phrase refers to the resident
reigner who had become the "permanent guest" of the clan
d to some extent shared its rights and duties. (A quite dif-
rent word describes the wholly detached foreigner, who oc-
pied a very different position as an "unnaturalized alien.")[3]
The slave occupied a much better position than the word
ggests to modern ears. As his master's property, he was in
more dependent condition than that of the protected
trangers"; on the other hand, the more intimate relations of
e slave to a particular family gave him a more assured posi-
n and evoked particular interests on his behalf. A foreign
ve could be held for life, but the servitude of a Hebrew
ve was limited to six years, and the earliest code of Hebrew
w contemplates his saying at the end of that period, "I love
y master, my wife, and my children; I will not go out free"
Exod. 21:5). Such a slave might become a trusted friend,
ke him whom Abraham sent to his kinsfolk in Aram to
oose a wife for Isaac.
We have been thinking so far of the smaller local group,
ith which the individual stood in closest relation. Beyond
is was the tribal association of such clans, usually occupying

[3] ["Stranger within thy gates," "sojourner" (R.S.V.), as at Exod. 20:10,
in Hebrew *gēr;* for the foreigner or "unnaturalized alien" a different
ord, *zār*, is used (R.S.V., "outsider," as at Exod. 29:33), or *nokri*,
oreigner," as at Gen. 31:15.—EDITOR.]

a common geographical area, which had its own particul[ar]
interests. But, beyond this again, was the largest and mo[st]
important unity, that of Israel. However mixed in blood [its]
original elements were, and however strong the disintegrati[ng]
influences of a country which has well been called "a land [of]
tribes" rather than the land of a united nation, the natio[nal]
unity became a most important fact for the history of Isra[el.]
It is characteristic of the genius and eventual contribution [of]
Israel that this national unity was from the outset based [on]
religion. It has already been suggested that not all the lat[er]
"Israelites" went down to Egypt and returned to inva[de]
Canaan, but that some of them had long since settled the[re.]
Be this as it may, it was the Josephites (as we may call t[he]
Egyptian contingent) who were destined to form the nucle[us]
of the future nation. They were welded into an aggressi[ve]
unity sufficient to force their way into parts of Canaan [by]
their faith in Yahweh as their war-god. That which ma[de]
Him different from the war-gods of other similar Semit[ic]
groups was their wonderful escape from the Egyptians und[er]
His leadership and the light which this escape threw on H[is]
nature and purpose. He was believed to have freely chos[en]
this particular group for Himself and to require from it [a]
fidelity doubtless crude and limited enough in detail, but mo[ral]
in spirit. Yahweh was forever "the out-of-Egypt bringi[ng]
God" (as a German might phrase it); Israel was the chos[en]
people, linked to him by no quasi-physical tie such as that [of]
a nature-God, but by a moral act. It was this relation whi[ch]
(under changing forms and details of expression) underl[ay]
the covenant of Yahweh with his people. The relation [of]
moral obligation as well as of feeling has a special na[me]
(*ḥesed*) in Hebrew, which is inadequately translated as "lo[v]-
ing-kindness." It means much the same as *agápē* in the Ne[w]
Testament. Observe that the covenant is with the nation, n[ot]
with the individual Israelites except as members or represent[a]-
tives of the nation. Throughout the whole period of the O[ld]
Testament, this covenant with the "corporate personality" [of]
Israel (as we may call it) remains the all-inclusive fact a[nd]

26

ctor, whatever the increase in the consciousness of individ-
lity.

Two examples will make this conception clearer. They may
taken from two of the greatest poems of the Old Testament
erature. One of them, the Song of Deborah [Judg. 5], is
r earliest document for the history of Israel. The other,
e Song of the Servant [Isa. 42:1-4, 49:1-6, 50:4-9, and 52:13
3:12], closes the era of the great prophets, and forms the
lminating glory of Old Testament religion. In both there
he unitary conception of the corporate personality of Israel.
In the Song of Deborah we hear of the danger in which
e scattered groups of Israel stood from the pressure of the
naanites. The Israelites are not simply scattered geographi-
ly; they are disunited in interest. Judah, Simeon, and Levi
e not mentioned, probably because they had no tribal exis-
ce at this time, i.e., a generation or two after the first
trance of the Josephites into Canaan. The Song praises
ose who came to the help of Yahweh, viz., Issachar, Zebulun,
phtali, Machir-Manasseh, Ephraim, and Benjamin. It blames
erely those who stood aloof, viz., Reuben, Gilead-Gad,
n, and Asher. (These all dwelt at a greater distance from
e plain where the battle was fought, which meant that their
mediate interests were not so much at stake.) Perhaps this
s the first great occasion of common action in Canaan, and
e significant thing for us is that the unity is defined simply
a common loyalty to Yahweh, who came from his mountain
me in the south as the storm-god to help his people Israel
n their battle through storm and flood:

The stars in their courses fought against Sisera,
The river Kishon swept them away.

(Judges 5:20-21).

er against this battle-song of the earliest days, we may set
Songs of the Servant of the Lord, particularly that of
ah 53. It represents Israel in her corporate personality,
el going down to national death in exile, yet to be divinely

27

raised in a national restoration to her former home. T'
prophet hears the future confession of the nations of the eart
when they behold that resurrection and see how they ha'
misjudged this people. That which seemed divine penalty f
sin is now seen as vicarious suffering for the nations, a sac:
ficial offering through which *they* may approach the God
Israel. Between the militant passion of the Song of Debor
and the sacrificial passion of the Song of the Servant, a who
world of religious development lies; but it is throughout t
group conception of Israel that is primary. In both Songs, t
individual has, of course, his place, whether Deborah a:
Barak and Jael, or the unknown prophet of the exile who
calling for a religious consciousness in all Israelites like 1
own. But in both we see that it is the group which occup:
the foreground of thought and feeling, since Yahweh is alwa
the covenanted God of *Israel*.

2

THE EMERGENCE OF THE INDIVIDUAL
THROUGH THE PROPHETIC CONSCIOUSNE:

It was characteristic that the national unity of Israel shou
have been created and sustained by its religion. It was equa'
characteristic that the fuller sense of individuality should
a product of the prophetic consciousness. This fuller ser
came through the religious experience of men who believ
that they stood in an individual relation both to God and t
nation. They were the eyes of the people toward God a:
the mouth of God toward the people (Isa. 29:10, Jer. 15:1'
From their individual call onward, their experience and the
message alike isolated them in greater or less degree; thus t
prophet Jeremiah cries to God, "I sat not in the assembly
them that make merry, nor rejoiced: I sat alone because
thy hand" (15:17). No man can be forced into such isolati
from the natural fellowships of life without one of two thir
happening. Either he will become sullen and embittered,

lse he will find consolation and compensation in a deeper
ense of God. The God of Israel was always conceived as a
'erson, and there is no surer way of deepening our own per-
onality than fellowship with a greater one. In discovering
vhat the greater personality is, we discover our own. The
rocess by which the prophet came to reflect the thought and
eeling of God exalted him into a new consciousness of in-
ividual worth to God. This initial factor made the prophets
ioneers of a richer sense of individual personality and able to
:ave behind them a legacy which has become part of the
piritual inheritance of the world.

But the initial factor, their own relation to God, was rein-
orced by the very demands they made of Israel in the name
f God. "Cease to do evil, learn to do well; seek justice, make
he violent keep straight; give judgment for the orphan,
upport the cause of the widow" (Isa. 1:16-17). Their mes-
age was to the nation, but they asked justice and mercy from
he individual Israelite toward his neighbor as the true and
ssential fulfilment of God's desires, without which the ritual
f worship became a mockery. This social ethic was the
irect development of the old nomadic clan spirit, purified and
nlightened, and raised to the level of a religious offering to
God. The corporate personality of Israel could not stand in
right relation to God unless it approached Him in this unity
f internal and individual fellowship. Such a demand, so con-
eived, even when presented to the nation, became inevitably
demand for an *individual* response to it. Moreover, it
ecame increasingly a demand for something more than the
xternal reformation of conduct. Hosea saw that what was
/rong with Israel was its inner spirit of infidelity (4:12, 5:4).
he only fulfilment of God's law was love. The book of
)euteronomy, largely influenced by Hosea's teaching, pro-
laimed, "Thou shalt love Yahweh thy God" (6:5), and justi-
ed the paradox of a law to love by presenting Yahweh as a
vable, because a redeeming, God (6:21 ff.). Jeremiah,
ying, "Thou art near in their mouth and far from their
ffections" (12:2), is contrasting the common shout of praise

with the individual motive to thanksgiving. This new em
phasis on motive went far to individualize the relation of th
Israelite to Yahweh.

But the religious experience of the prophets went farthe
still in this process of individualization. They were themselve
sustained in their mission by the personal fellowship of Goc
the experience of which one of them wrote, "morning b
morning He wakeneth mine ear to hear as a disciple" (Is;
50:4). Some of them came to see that they were making
demand on the individual Israelites which could be fulfille
only by divine aid, God's acts of individualizing grace. S
we have the promise of a "new covenant" through Jeremial
which should be individualized and internalized, in contras
with all previous covenants which had been national and e>
pressed in external forms: "I will put my law in their inwar
parts, and in their heart will I write it" (31:31 ff.). It is sti
a covenant "with the house of Israel," but it is accomplishe
through a new and more searching relation of God to eac
member of that house. So also with the promise of grac
through Jeremiah's younger contemporary, Ezekiel (36:2(
27): "A new heart will I give you, and a new spirit will
put within you; and I will take away the stony heart out o
your flesh, and I will give you a heart of flesh. And I wi
put my spirit within you, and cause you to walk in m
statutes."

This new individualization of the relation of Israel to Go
is confirmed by the fact that Ezekiel (chap. 18) proclaim
individual moral responsibility in sharper terms than anyon
before him. 'The soul that sinneth, *it* shall die"—not othe⟩
also, as the older conception of corporate personality ha
demanded from Achan's family (Josh. 7:24 ff.).

If we think of the prophets of Israel as a spiritual ari⟨
tocracy, then we may say that what they hoped for was
democratization of their own relation to God, when all th
Lord's people would be prophets (Num. 11:29), and Go
would pour out his spirit upon all flesh (Joel 2:28). Indee⟨
we may say in general of the "great men" of Israel, tho⟨

itstanding personalities which are so prominent in her his-
ry, that they are what they are precisely in this way. Their
iman personality is again and again shown to be achieved
a response to the call and influence of divine personality.
might well be argued, even on purely philosophical grounds,
iat no profounder interpretation of human personality could
er be given.

3

THE SYNTHESES MADE BY JUDAISM AND CHRISTIANITY

From this religious individualism *within* the still retained
oup-consciousness there came in course of time a twofold
nthesis, viz., that of Judaism and that of Christianity. We
ay draw a homely illustration from the lump of coal. Be-
nd the coal seam there lies the long perspective of primeval
rests and luxuriant vegetation which have lived and died
create it. The coal itself will yield both gas and coke, each
oduct bringing its own chain of industrial developments.
we may think of the religion of Israel ultimately deposit-
g the literature of the Old Testament, which has become
e source of two great religions, viz., Judaism and Chris-
inity, each with its far-reaching influence on the history
the world.

The new synthesis of individual Israelites which we call
idaism becomes visible only after the exile and the return of
me of the exiles. But the synthesis of those individuals who
ere to shape a new future really began with such a group
the disciples who gathered round Isaiah (Isa. 8:16). Such
llowship is seen again and again, notably in the pious circles
om which many of the psalms came, and in the group of
hich we hear in the book of Malachi: "Then they that
ared the Lord spake one with another: and the Lord heark-
ied and heard, and a book of remembrance was written be-
re him, for them that feared the Lord and that thought

upon his name" (3:16). We have their spiritual descendant
in the Hasidim, those enthusiasts for the Jewish Law wh
supported Judas Maccabeus (I Macc. 2:42) so long as h
was fighting for religious liberty (7:13). From these agai
came the Pharisees, those religious leaders of the ordinar
people who were destined to shape its religious future an
to remain supreme as the rabbis of the Mishnah and Talmud
after the Jewish War had eliminated their chief rivals, the Sad
ducees. It is important to realize that this was a new synthesi
and not merely the post-exilic continuation of pre-exilic Israe
Those who did return from exile were the chosen few wh
had learned from the prophets that repentance was fundamenta
in any right relation to God. The ritual of the Temple, an
later, the legalism of the Torah might limit or modify th
spirituality of this individual relation to God but by no mear
destroyed it. Further, we find that the most important and in
fluential change of doctrine, the belief in a real life beyon
death, which was absent from the religion of Israel and was de
veloped in Judaism, is itself necessarily a belief concerning th
individual. Not all Gentiles would be excluded from, an
not all Jews would be admitted to, that future life. Th
nation remained—and remains still for the Jew—as a fact an
as a privilege, an individual opportunity, not a guarantee, c
blessedness and resurrection from the dead.

The Christian synthesis was affiliated to the same line c
development of the religious group within the nation:
group, but it emphasized the prophetic and apocalypti
rather than the legalistic and moralistic features of tha
development, whilst sharing in the Jewish hope of lif
beyond death. The new fact, the crystallizing center fc
Judaism, had been the Torah, the Law ascribed to Mose
both written (the Pentateuch) and unwritten ("the traditio
of the elders," Mark 7:3). The present arrangement of th
Old Testament literature reflects the later belief of Judaisn
which turned the literary result of the whole developmer
into a revelation given to Moses on Sinai. In that sense th
Old Testament is a Jewish book, whereas the Christian a

ngement might have been a different one (had change then
een possible), giving primacy to the prophets. The new
ict for Christianity was not a Book, but a Person. Jesus
ame as the Jewish Prophet-Messiah, but completely trans-
ormed the title by preferring the transcendent and apoca-
yptic to the political and nationalistic idea, and blending
vith it the conception of the suffering Servant of the Lord.
Around him a new group formed, that of his immediate
isciples, a new Israel of God.

St. Paul has shown us this group at a further stage of its
evelopment, using the metaphor of the body of Christ. Here
ve see the new synthesis in clearest form, especially if we
iterpret the metaphor, as we should, by Hebrew and not by
Greek psychology. In the Hebrew conception, the body,
ot the soul, is the essential personality; the body is indeed
nimated by the soul, in each of its members, but then each
f these, by a sort of diffused consciousness, shares in the
sychical and ethical, as well as in the physical, life of the
ody. Thus St. Paul (I Cor. 12:12 ff.) is led to conceive
nose who are spiritually gathered round Christ by faith in
im as members of his body. They vary in function and rank,
ut they are made one by the unity of the body, animated
s it is by the one Spirit of the Lord. This is the most explicit
tterance of the Bible concerning the relation of the group
nd the individual. It implies a new kind of individual, but
ne who, like the true Israelite of old, could never be divorced
rom his social relationship.

Other lecturers in this series [4] have reminded us that the
elation of the group to the individual is a present-day issue,
nd have indicated the bearing of their study of the past
pon the present. What might be learned from our review
f the emergence of the individual in Israel? First, that all
rogress comes through individual initiative and through the

---

[4] [Undergraduate lectures at Oxford in 1936 on "The Individual in
ast and West"; see Introduction, p. xi.—EDITOR.]

action of a minority. Israel's history has contributed so great
to religion partly because it was the history of a communi
in which there was so much scope and freedom for the ind
vidual life. This was in no small degree due to the dem
cratic traditions of the desert, which persisted long in Canaa
T. E. Lawrence says truly of the Semitic races, "They we
a people of spasms, of upheavals, of ideas, the race of tl
individual genius." [5] "The Semites' idea of nationality w
the independence of clans and villages." [6] So the history
Israel is largely the story of its great individuals, pioneers
the discovery of religious truth—Moses, Elijah, Amos, Hose
Isaiah, Jeremiah, and Deutero-Isaiah. Freedom for individu
utterance remains the essential condition of national progres
as our own Milton so vigorously pleaded in his *Areopagitic*

In the second place, the progress made by Israel to a larg
truth was conditioned by a lively faith in the spiritual an
unseen world, for which its great individuals became tl
spokesmen. Without such loyalty to something greater ar
more lasting than the passing fashions of thought in a sing
generation, there can be no lasting gain, even if there is gai
at all. Graham Wallas, in his classical book, *The Great Sc
ciety*, after speaking of the value and necessity of individu
initiative, rightly goes on to say, "Napoleon on the Imperi
throne, the financial genius when he has overcome his rival
the leader of young opinion when his books are read and h
plays acted in twenty languages, may create nothing but cor
fusion and weakness unless his power is related to son
greater purpose, in whose service is liberty." [7] Mere civiliza
tion and culture without religion become as perilous as di
the culture of Canaan to Israel's historic purpose and destin
In fact, there is some truth in the pessimistic words of a Ru
sian thinker, Rostovtzeff: "Is not every civilization bound t

[5] *Seven Pillars of Wisdom* (Garden City, New York: Doubleda
Doran, and Co., 1935), p. 39.

[6] *Ibid.*, p. 100.

[7] *The Great Society: a Psychological Analysis* (New York: Ma
millan, 1914), p. 83.

cay as soon as it begins to penetrate the masses?" [8] De-
)cracy is too often like the loud-speaker which coarsens the
ice and may make it unrecognizable. Popularization, even
 religious truth, means some compromise of its truthful-
ss. There is always need of the individual, who endures in
: strength of the vision he has seen, and endures in the often
grateful task of urging the valley crowd to climb the
ights with him. It is religion alone, in one form or another,
uich can make—not the world safe for democracy, but de-
)cracy safe for the world.

As quoted in J. L. and B. Hammond, *The Bleak Age* ("Swan
•rary," 26; New York: Longmans, 1934), p. vi.

For Further Reading

By H. WHEELER ROBINSON

Deuteronomy and Joshua, Vol. IV in "The Century Bible," ε
W. F. ADENEY. Edinburgh: T. C. & E. C. Jack, 1907.

"Hebrew Psychology in Relation to Pauline Anthropology,"
*Mansfield College Essays Presented to the Reverend Andrε
Martin Fairbairn, D.D. on the occasion of his Seventieth Birt
day, November 4, 1908.* London: Hodder and Stoughton, 19ϵ
Pp. 265-86.

"Baptist Principles before the rise of Baptist Churches," in *T*
Baptists of Yorkshire (1911), pp. 3-50. Reprinted as *Bapt*
Principles ("Christian Education Manuals"). London: King
gate Press, 1925; third ed., 1938. Paperback ed., Greenwoϲ
S. C.: Attic Press, 1955. German trans., 1931; Danish tran
1939.

The Christian Doctrine of Man. Edinburgh: T & T. Clark, 19ⁱ
Second ed., 1913; third ed., 1926.

The Religious Ideas of the Old Testament ("Studies in Theology
24). London: Duckworth, 1913. Second ed., rev. by L. ⅰ
BROCKINGTON; London: Duckworth, and Naperville: Allensϲ
1956.

The Cross of Job. London: SCM, 1916. Second rev. ed., "Religⁱ
and Life Books," 1938.

The Cross of Jeremiah. London: SCM, 1925.

The Cross of the Servant. London: SCM, 1926.

The Cross in the Old Testament. London: SCM, 1955, and Phiⁱ
delphia: Westminster, 1956. Reprints *The Cross of Job* (191ϲ
pp. 9-54; *The Cross of the Servant* (1926), pp. 55-114; and *T*
Cross of Jeremiah (1925), pp. 115-92, though the original aⁱ
pendices and bibliographies are omitted.

"Hebrew Psychology," in *The People and the Book*, ed. A. ⅰ
PEAKE. Oxford University Press, 1925. Pp. 353-82.

be Life and Faith of the Baptists ("The Faiths" series). London: Methuen, 1927, Greenwood, S. C.: Attic Press, 1946.

be Christian Experience of the Holy Spirit ("The Library of Constructive Theology"). London: Nisbet, and New York: Harper, 1928. Seventh ed., 1940.

be Veil of God ("The New Library of Devotion"). London: Nisbet, 1936.

"he Old Testament Background," in *Christian Worship: Studies in its History and Meaning*, ed. N. Micklem. Oxford University Press, 1936. Pp. 19-34.

"he Christian Doctrine of Redemption," in *The Christian Faith*, ed. W. R. Matthews. London: Eyre & Spottiswoode, 1936. Pp. 209-31.

be Old Testament: its Making and Meaning. University of London Press, and Nashville: Cokesbury, 1937.

be History of Israel: its Facts and Factors ("Studies in Theology," 42). London: Duckworth, 1938 (now in its ninth printing). Paperback ed., Naperville: Allenson, 1956.

ecord and Revelation: Essays on the Old Testament by Members of the Society for Old Testament Study, ed. H. Wheeler Robinson. Oxford: Clarendon Press, 1938. Includes Robinson's essay, "The Theology of the Old Testament (The Philosophy of Revelation and The Characteristic Doctrines)," pp. 303-48.

..aw and Religion in Israel," in *Judaism and Christianity*, ed. E. I. J. Rosenthal. London: Sheldon Press, and New York: Macmillan, 1937-38. Vol. III (1938), pp. 45-66.

uffering, Human and Divine ("Great Issues of Life" series). London: SCM, and New York: Macmillan, 1939.

The Religion of Israel," in *A Companion to the Bible*, ed. T. W. Manson. Edinburgh: T. & T. Clark, 1939. Pp. 287-331.

he Bible in its Ancient and English Versions, ed. H. Wheeler Robinson. Oxford: Clarendon Press, 1940. Includes two essays by Robinson, "The Hebrew Bible," pp. 1-38, and "The Bible as the Word of God," pp. 275-302.

edemption and Revelation in the Actuality of History ("The Library of Constructive Theology"). London: Nisbet, 1942.

spiration and Revelation in the Old Testament. Oxford: Clarendon Press, 1946. ("Speaker's Lectures" at Oxford, 1942-45, presenting a prolegomena for Robinson's proposed Old Testa-

ment theology. Now available in an Oxford University Pr
paperback.)

The Cross of Hosea, ed. E. A. PAYNE. Philadelphia: Westmins
1949. (See next title.)

Two Hebrew Prophets: Studies in Hosea and Ezekiel, ed. E.
PAYNE. London: Lutterworth Press, 1959, and Naperville: .
lenson, 1962. (Lectures from 1935 and 1943 respectively; th
on Hosea were published separately in the United States
1949, as noted above).

About H. Wheeler Robinson

PAYNE, ERNEST A. *Henry Wheeler Robinson, Scholar, Teach
Principal: A Memoir.* London: Nisbet, 1946. In addition to
biographical memoir (pp. 9-109), a selected bibliography, a
portrait of Robinson, seven of his previously unpublished l
tures are included.

_____. *Studies in History and Religion Presented to
H. Wheeler Robinson, M.A., on his seventieth birthd.*
London: Lutterworth, 1942. A full portrait and a more detai
bibliography are included; the bibliography lists articles
commentaries, dictionaries, and encyclopedias, but by no me:
all his articles for popular journals nor his book reviews.

About Corporate Personality and Related Topics

For Robinson's later remarks, see especially *Record and Reve
tion,* pp. 332 f.; *Redemption and Revelation,* pp. 149 f., 246, 2
62, 281 f., 287-89; and *Inspiration and Revelation,* pp. 70 f.,
85, 169 f., and 264.

JOHNSON, AUBREY R. *The One and the Many in the Israelite Cc
ception of God.* Cardiff: University of Wales Press, 19
²1961. Especially pp. 1-22.

_____. *The Vitality of the Individual in the Thought
Ancient Israel.* Cardiff: University of Wales Press, 1949.
83, n. 2, and 102, n. 2. Johnson disputes Wheeler Robinso
view about "diffusion of consciousness" (whereby limbs or
gans of the body seem to function independently) and expla
such Old Testament passages as synecdoche.

JACOB, EDMOND. *Theology of the Old Testament.* Translated
ARTHUR W. HEATHCOTE and PHILIP J. ALLCOCK. London: Hc
der and Stoughton, and New York: Harper, 1958. Pp. 153-5

For Further Reading

: Servant

RTH, CHRISTOPHER R. *The Suffering Servant in Deutero-Isaiah: n Historical and Critical Study.* Oxford University Press,)48; ²1956. Pp. 3 f., 103-16, 202-7; cf. p. 210, n. 2.

_____. "Servant of the Lord, The," in *The Interpreter's Dic-onary of the Bible.* New York: Abingdon, 1962. Vol. IV, pp.)2-94.

OLOM, JOH. *The Servant Songs in Deutero-Isaiah: A New ttempt to Solve an Old Problem.* Lund: C. W. K. Gleerup,)51. P. 103.

ISER, ARTUR. *The Old Testament: Its Formation and Develop-ent.* New York: Association Press, 1961. Pp. 200-04 on aeories about the Servant.

HRODT, WALTHER. *Theology of the Old Testament, Volume ne.* Translated by J. A. BAKER. "The Old Testament Li-rary." Philadelphia: Westminster, 1961. On p. 483, n. 4, the corporate personality" theory is rejected.

he Psalms

ISER, ARTUR. *The Psalms: A Commentary.* Translation by IERBERT HARTWELL. Philadelphia: Westminster, 1962. See pp. 5-72, 80-81, and 91, on "laments of the individual" and the "I" f the Psalms.

w Testament Applications

NSON, T. W. *The Servant Messiah: A Study of the Public 1inistry of Jesus.* Cambridge University Press, 1953. Pp. 73 f. aperback reprint, 1961.

BINSON, JOHN A. T. *The Body: A Study in Pauline Theology* "Studies in Biblical Theology," No. 5). Chicago: Henry Regnery, 1952. Pp. 55-67; cf. 14.

Facet Books

Titles already published:

1. *The Significance of the Bible for the Church*
   by Anders Nygren (translated by Carl C. Rasmussen)
   1963
2. *The Sermon on the Mount*
   by Joachim Jeremias (translated by Norman Perrin). 196
3. *The Old Testament in the New*
   by C. H. Dodd. 1963
4. *The Literary Impact of the Authorized Version*
   by C. S. Lewis. 1963
5. *The Meaning of Hope*
   by C. F. D. Moule. 1963
6. *Biblical Problems and Biblical Preaching*
   by C. K. Barrett. 1964
7. *The Genesis Accounts of Creation*
   by Claus Westermann (translated by Norman E. Wagner)
   1964
8. *The Lord's Prayer*
   by Joachim Jeremias (translated by John Reumann)
   1964
9. *Only to the House of Israel? Jesus and the Non-Jews*
   by T. W. Manson. 1964
10. *Jesus and the Wilderness Community at Qumran*
    by Ethelbert Stauffer (translated by Hans Spalteholz)
    1964
11. *Corporate Personality in Ancient Israel*
    by H. Wheeler Robinson. 1964
12. *The Sacrifice of Christ*
    by C. F. D. Moule. 1964
13. *The Problem of the Historical Jesus*
    by Joachim Jeremias (translated by Norman Perrin). 196